HITTING
THE
BOOKS
Skills for Reading, Writing, and Research

Writing an Opinion Paper

Meg Greve

Rourke
Educational Media

rourkeeducationalmedia.com

*Scan for Related Titles
and Teacher Resources*

Before Reading:

Building Academic Vocabulary and Background Knowledge

Before reading a book, it is important to tap into what your child or students already know about the topic. This will help them develop their vocabulary, increase their reading comprehension, and make connections across the curriculum.

1. *Look at the cover of the book. What will this book be about?*
2. *What do you already know about the topic?*
3. *Let's study the Table of Contents. What will you learn about in the book's chapters?*
4. *What would you like to learn about this topic? Do you think you might learn about it from this book? Why or why not?*
5. *Use a reading journal to write about your knowledge of this topic. Record what you already know about the topic and what you hope to learn about the topic.*
6. *Read the book.*
7. *In your reading journal, record what you learned about the topic and your response to the book.*
8. *After reading the book complete the activities below.*

Content Area Vocabulary
Read the list. What do these words mean?

audience
brainstorming
hook
persuade
research
strategy
supported
synonyms
visual
voice

After Reading:

Comprehension and Extension Activity

After reading the book, work on the following questions with your child or students in order to check their level of reading comprehension and content mastery.

1. *What is the purpose of an opinion paper? (Summarize)*
2. *Why is research important when writing an opinion paper? (Infer)*
3. *What methods do you use to convince someone of your opinion? (Text to self connection)*
4. *Besides an opinion paper, what other forms might persuasion take? (Summarize)*
5 *Describe the format of an opinion paper. (Visualize)*

Extension Activity

Find an opinion paper to read on your own. How did the author support his or her argument? Did you agree or disagree? Write an opinion paper in response to the one you read.

Table of Contents

What Do You Think?

What is an **opinion**? What is a **fact**? A fact is something you can prove. An opinion is what you believe, usually **supported** by facts. Writing about an opinion seems like an easy task, but it may be more challenging than you think. We want everyone to agree with us because an opinion usually includes our feelings and emotions. The challenge is to appeal to other people's feelings and emotions, while leaving yours out.

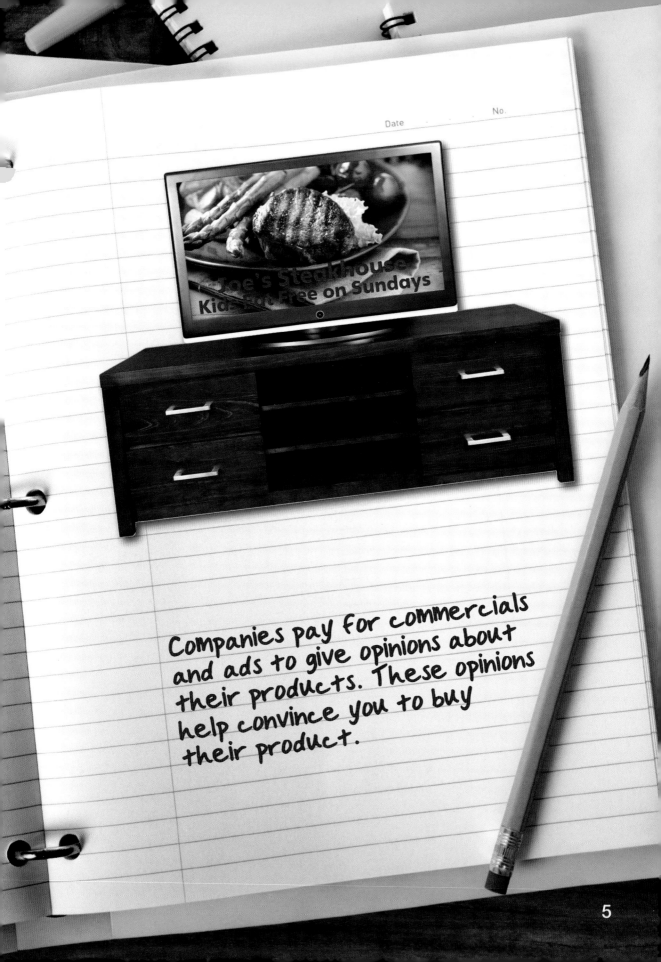

Companies pay for commercials and ads to give opinions about their products. These opinions help convince you to buy their product.

When writing an opinion paper, start with some pre-writing work to organize your thoughts. An easy way to do this is with a **brainstorming** chart. On a sheet of paper, create a list of as many reasons as you can that support your opinion.

Cafeteria needs bigger food menu

1. Option to try new foods
2. Healthy food choices

Instead of stating your opinion at the top of your paper, you can also write it in the center of your paper. This is easier to organize when you have details that support your reasons.

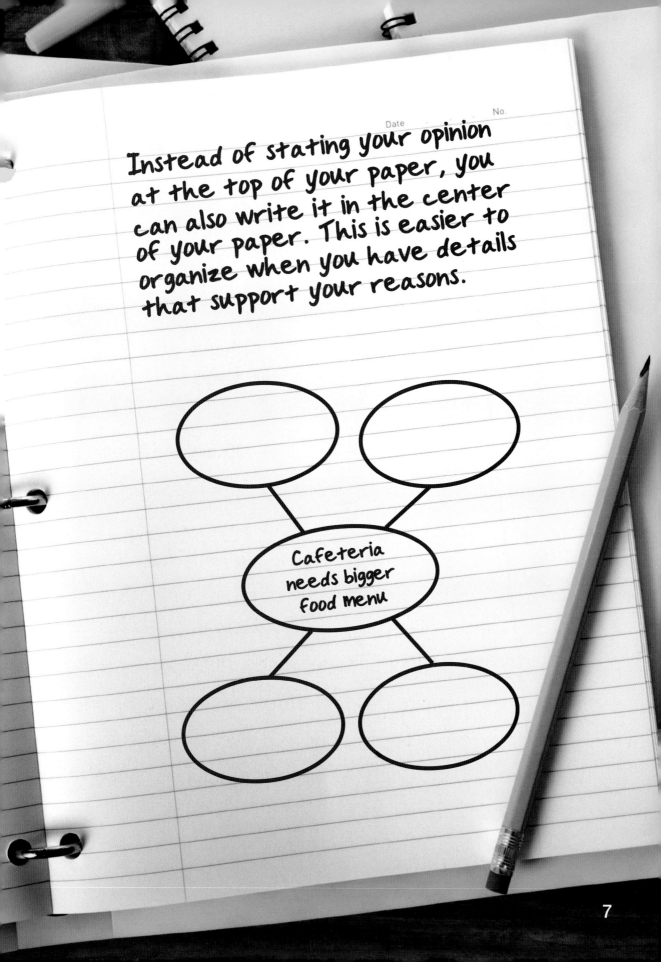

Cafeteria needs bigger food menu

Just the Facts

Opinions are personal. Yet, when you want someone to agree with your opinion, you cannot include your feelings. The best **strategy** to change someone's mind is to use facts. Reread your brainstorming list. Which reasons can be proven with facts and which are simply how you feel?

Circle the reasons that can be proven. Then number your opinions in order of most convincing to least convincing. Begin your **research** with the opinions that make the most sense. Find details that support your reasons. For example, if you are writing an opinion paper about why your soccer field should be improved, include the number of injuries caused by poor conditions.

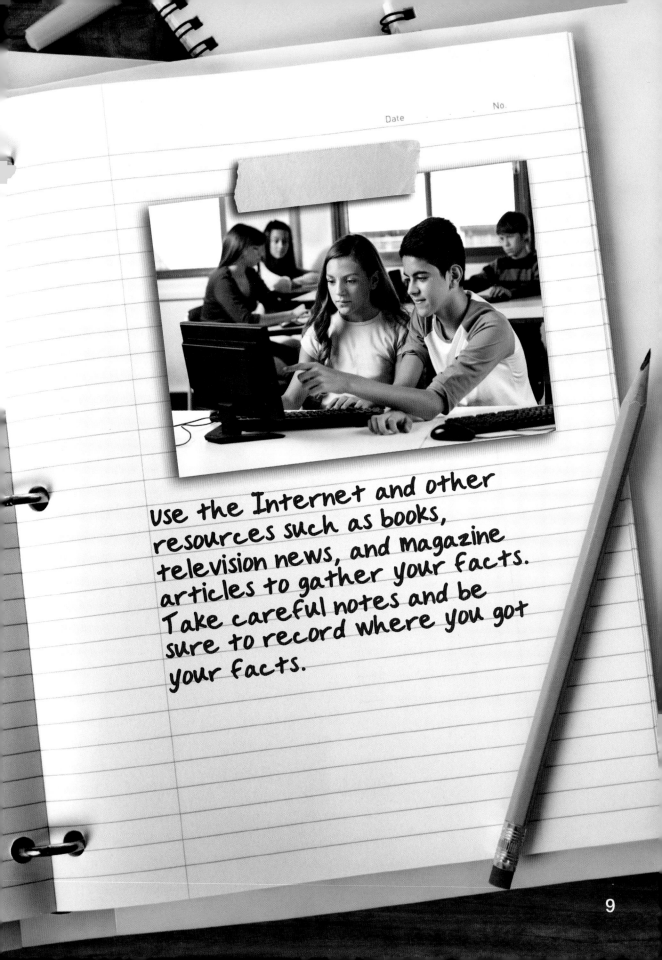

Use the Internet and other resources such as books, television news, and magazine articles to gather your facts. Take careful notes and be sure to record where you got your facts.

If you have a personal experience that strongly supports your point of view, include it in your paper. Personal stories are useful and effective arguments in an opinion paper. The reader will be able to connect to your story and see your point of view. Your reader may have even shared a similar experience.

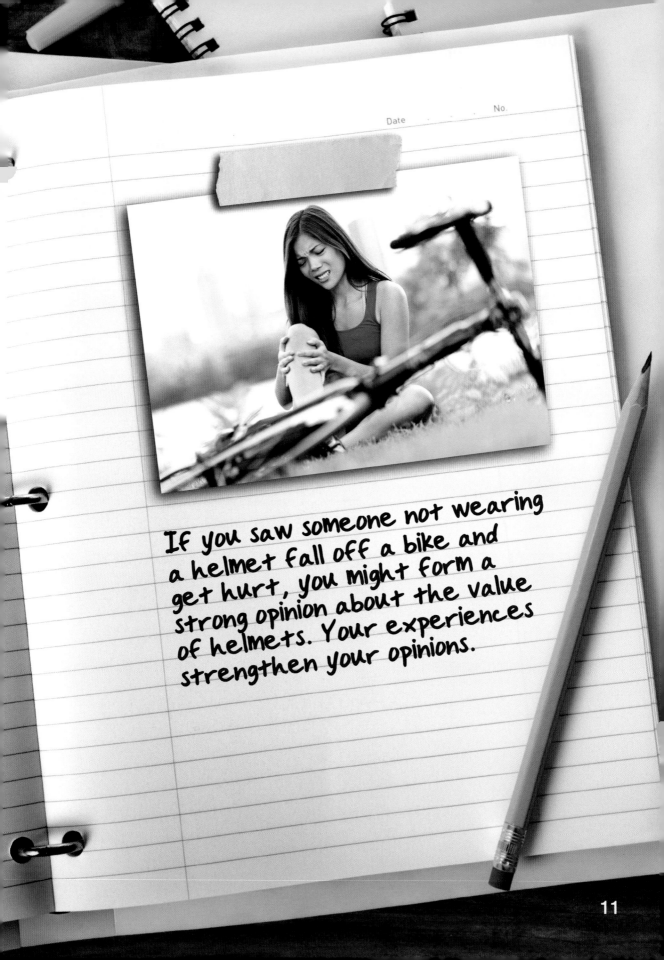

If you saw someone not wearing a helmet fall off a bike and get hurt, you might form a strong opinion about the value of helmets. Your experiences strengthen your opinions.

Formatting Your Paper

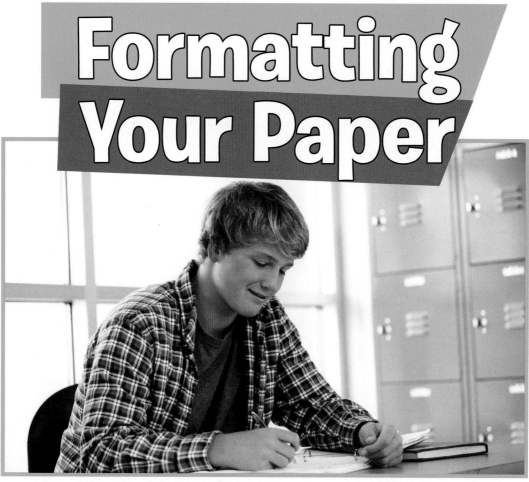

An opinion paper often has five paragraphs. The first paragraph includes a strong introduction. Start with a question or a fact that will **hook** readers into being interested in reading your opinion. One way to hook readers is by speaking to them directly. Use phrases such as, "Do you think . . ." or "Have you ever . . . ."

The introduction should also include a brief list of reasons for your opinion. But save the details for the other parts of the essay.

Format of an Opinion Paper

Paragraph 1:
Introduction

Paragraphs 2-4:
Reasons with details supporting your opinion.

Paragraph 5:
Closing paragraph summarizing your opinion and reasons.

Follow this format to create a strong opinion paper.

The next three paragraphs give the reasons and details supporting your opinion. While you are writing these paragraphs, consider your **audience**. Who will be reading your opinion? It might be the readers of your local newspaper, your classmates, or members of an online community. Think about what your audience needs to know and make that your focus. Use language and examples that appeal to your readers.

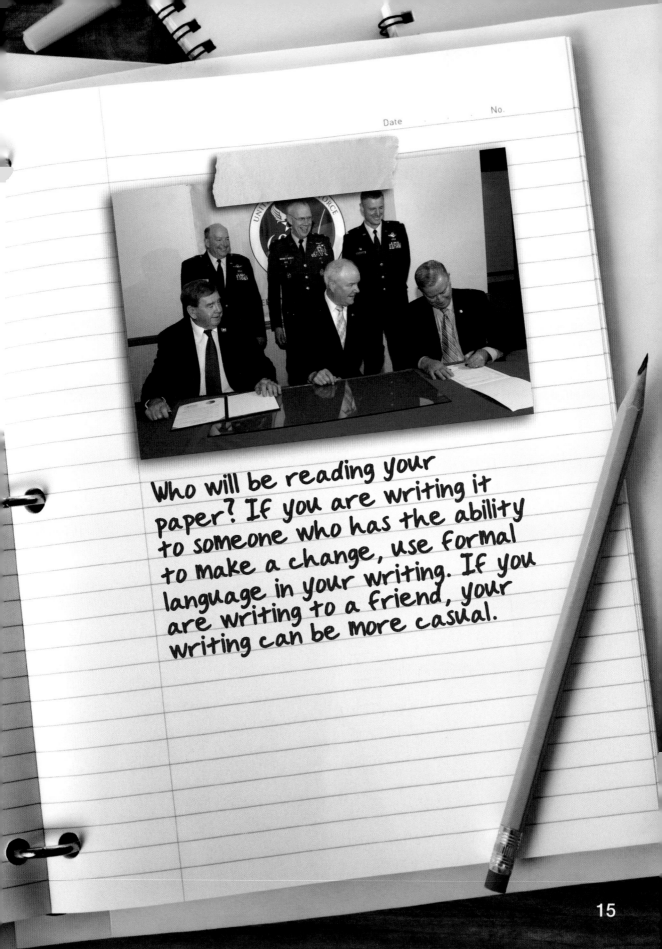

Who will be reading your paper? If you are writing it to someone who has the ability to make a change, use formal language in your writing. If you are writing to a friend, your writing can be more casual.

Make sure you use words and language that give a clear and strong **voice**. It is best to clearly state your opinion. Do not start with "I think . . . " or "In my opinion . . ." Use strong words and details supporting each reason.

While your audience is reading, they are forming their own opinions as well. They may even disagree with you. Think about why someone would not agree. Then, include an argument against your opinion. Start with a phrase like, "You might think . . ." or "It is true that . . ." Then explain why the opposing argument is wrong.

Useful Transition Words
First
Second
Third
One example
For example
In addition
For instance
Also
Finally

Transition words are important when writing an opinion paper. Using words such as first, next, or finally, keep the reader focused on your opinion.

Your final paragraph should restate your opinion and reasons supporting it. Try not to use the same words. Instead, use **synonyms** and similar examples. In some cases, you may even make a call to action. For example, if you are arguing in support of a recycling program at school, you may end with a plea for help, or a warning about negative consequences for not recycling.

Why the Cafeteria Needs a Bigger Menu

Introduction

I believe that our cafeteria should expand its lunch menu. With more options, students would be able to try new things, and access healthy food. Also, vegetarian students need more lunch options. For these reasons, I believe the cafeteria needs a bigger menu.

Reason 1

First, students should have the chance to try new foods. Many students just eat chicken fingers or bologna sandwiches every day. They need to try new food. My family eats tasty food from Mexico, China, and India. Students would enjoy tacos, lo mein, or naan if they got the chance to try it. It would also help them get interested in other cultures.

Reason 2

In addition, students need healthy food choices. Much of the cafeteria's current food is high in fat and sugar. When students eat this every day, it can cause them to gain weight or become unhealthy. If students had the choice to eat healthy food, they would be better off.

Reason 3

Finally, we need more vegetarian food in the cafeteria. Some students do not eat meat. Some days, there is nothing for them to eat in the cafeteria. They can only eat the tater tots and milk. This is not a good lunch. The cafeteria needs good food that these students can choose from.

Conclusion

In summary, I believe that the cafeteria needs to offer more food choices at lunch. More food choices will help students learn about new foods. It will let them learn how to make healthy food choices. It will also give vegetarians a way to get a full meal. If the cafeteria offers more food choices, all students will be happier and healthier.

The Art of Persuasion

Sometimes we want to **persuade** someone to agree with our opinion. Writing a paper that is well researched and well written is often the best form of persuasion. Other types of persuasion include speeches, advertisements, reviews, and commercials. These forms often include **visual** pieces. For example, someone arguing against pollution may make a poster with a photo of a factory blowing black smoke into the sky. A visual is a strong and effective way to explain your opinion.

Writing an opinion paper must be done carefully and thoughtfully. Remember to research your topic, use strong words, and include details in support of your argument. Your opinion matters; make sure others agree!

What is your opinion? You can use these ideas to write an opinion paper. Use what you learned to make yourself heard!

- We should have less homework.
- We should recycle at school and at home.
- I should have a cell phone.
- My bedtime should be later.
- We should not have school uniforms.
- Ice cream should be served at lunch.

Glossary

audience (AW-dee-uhnss): the person or people who are reading, watching, or listening

brainstorming (BRAYN-storm-ing): writing down as many ideas as possible

hook (HUK): an interesting phrase or sentence used to grab a reader's attention

persuade (per-SWADE): to convince someone of your opinion or belief

research (ri-SURCH): to learn and find out as much as you can on a topic

strategy (STRAT-uh-jee): a plan

supported (SUH-port-id): facts that helped strengthen an argument

synonyms (SIN-uh-nims): words that mean almost the same as other words

visual (VIZH-oo-uhl): something to be seen

voice (VOISS): the tone used in a piece of writing